DRAW patterns

with Barroux

BLUE  APPLE

THE PATTERNS

Have fun with these patterns in this book!

SQUARES!   TRIANGLES!
CIRCLES!

Finish the pattern here,

and here

DOTS

Finish the pattern.

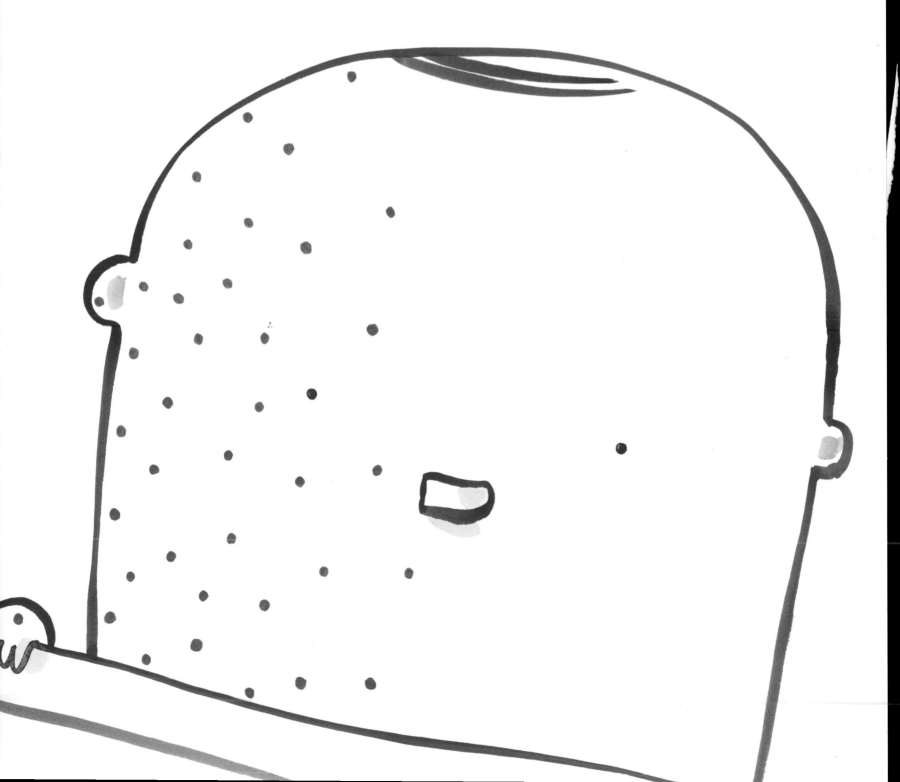

How many circles can you draw to make this pattern?

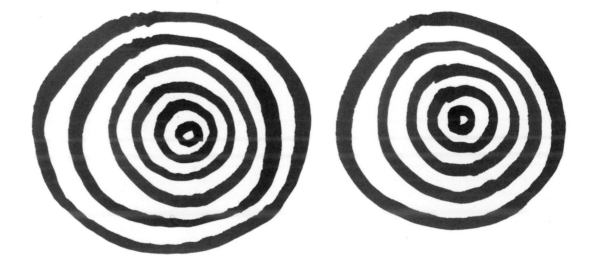

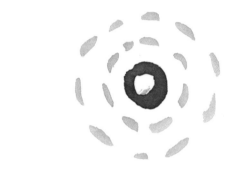

Copy and color the patterns.

WATER PATTERNS

Draw circles.

SPIRALS

Make a picture using these spinning spirals.

LOOPY LINES

Finish the loops and swoops all the way down the page.

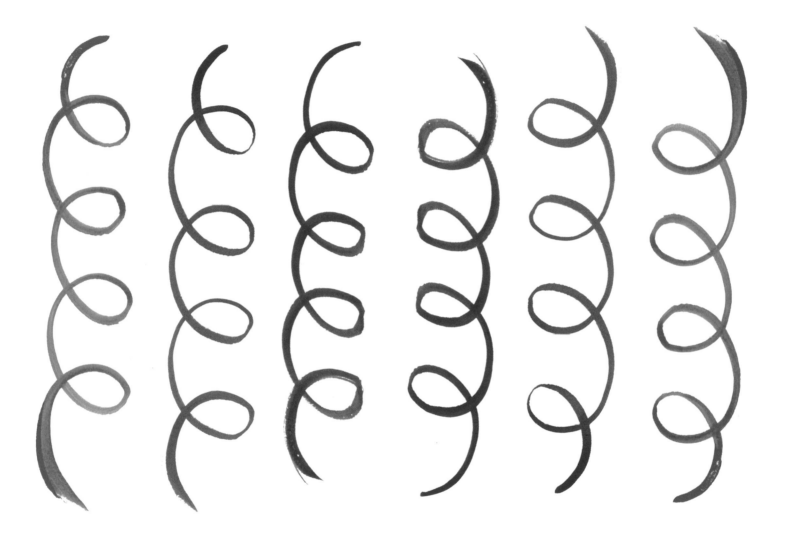

WAVES

Use your imagination.
Make a picture using these wavy lines.

CIRCLES

What can you make from these circles?

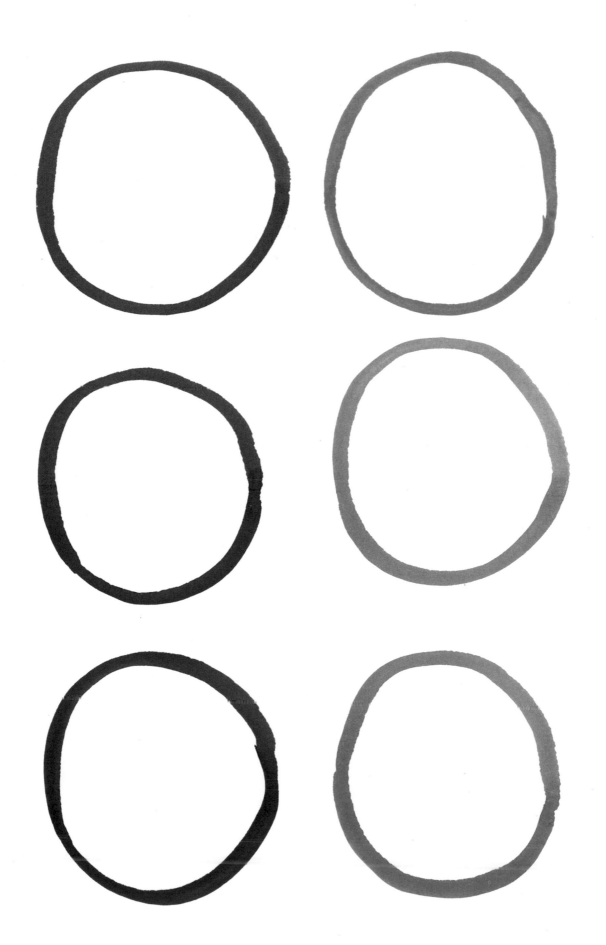

SNAP!

TRIANGLES

Every alligator needs teeth!
Make lots and lots of them.

Finish the pattern on Lily's party dress.

Add a scribbles pattern to each car.

Finish the pattern to make a rainy day!

Windows can make a pattern.
Draw more windows.

CURLICUE!
Draw lots and lots of curls.

Make fruit patterns.

**Use this wavy pattern
to fill the ocean!**

RECTANGLES

Draw windows
on these city buildings.

OCEAN WAVES

Finish the ocean waves.

What's under the sea?

SHORT LINES

Finish his fur!

BROKEN LINES

The flowers are
thirsty. Draw
more water.

Vines make patterns.
Draw more lines.

SPOTS

Use lots of circles to design the ladybugs.

STRIPES

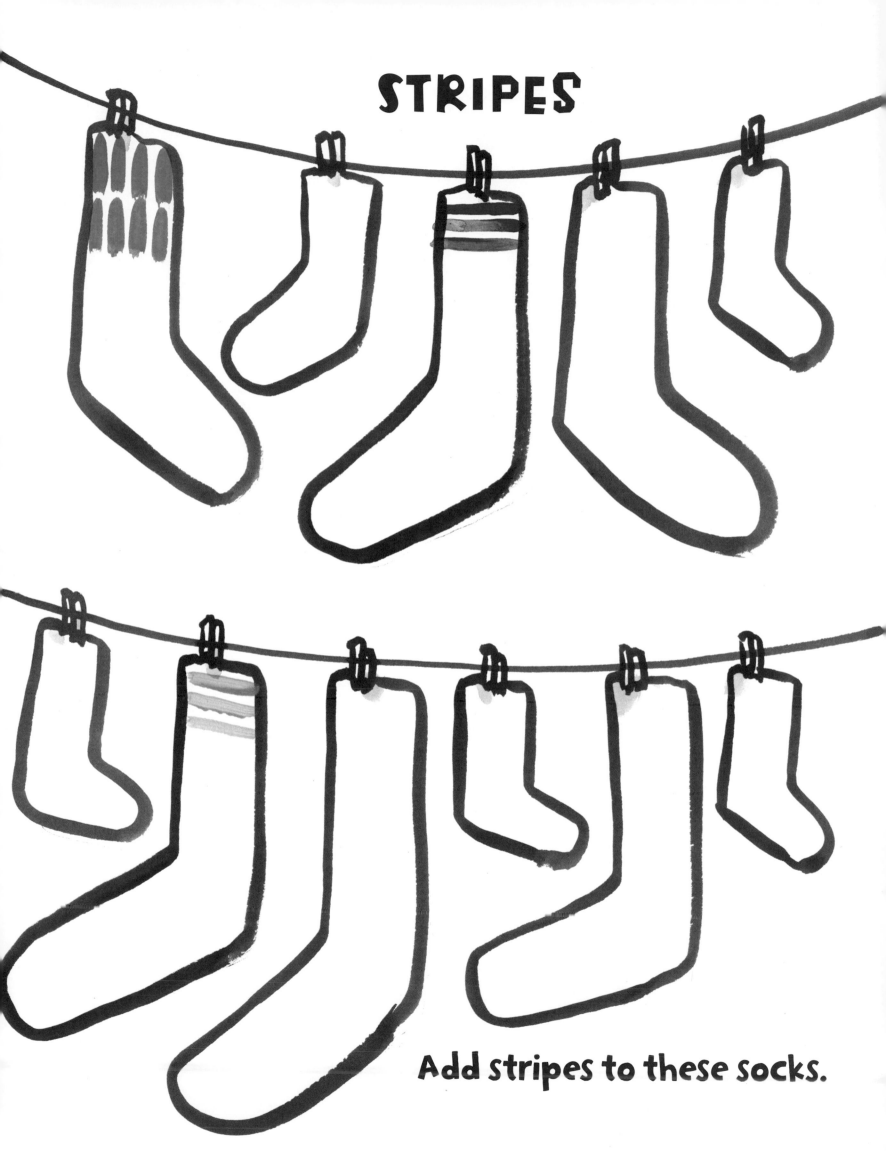

Add stripes to these socks.

SHORT LINES

Add bristles to the toothbrushes.

CURVY LINES

Add shingles to the roofs!

WAVY LINES

Add more tadpoles.

Don't forget to add water.

CURLY LINES

Add lines and follow the bees!

RAYS

**Add rays.
Light up the lights!**

BROKEN LINES

Draw dashes to
finish the roads.

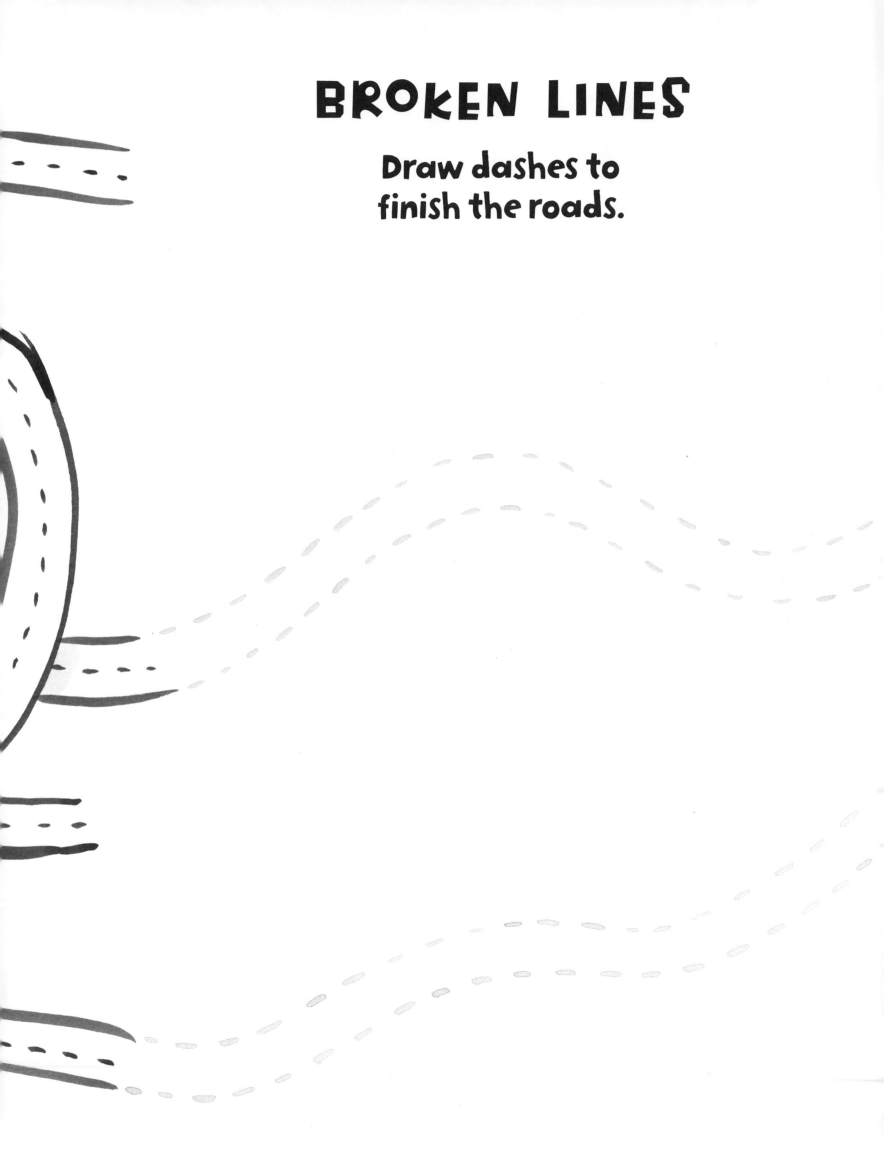

SPIRALS

Add tails.

STRIPES

Turn these horses into zebras. Add stripes!

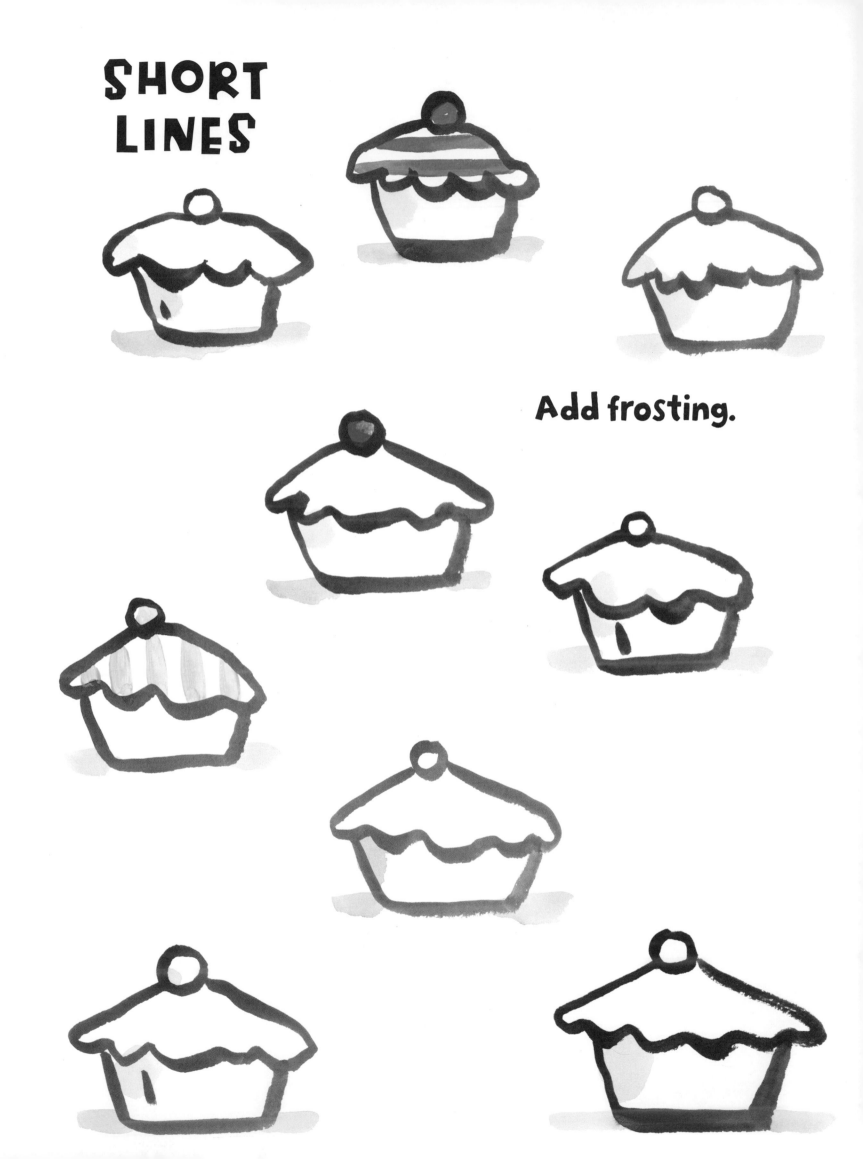

SHORT LINES

Add frosting.

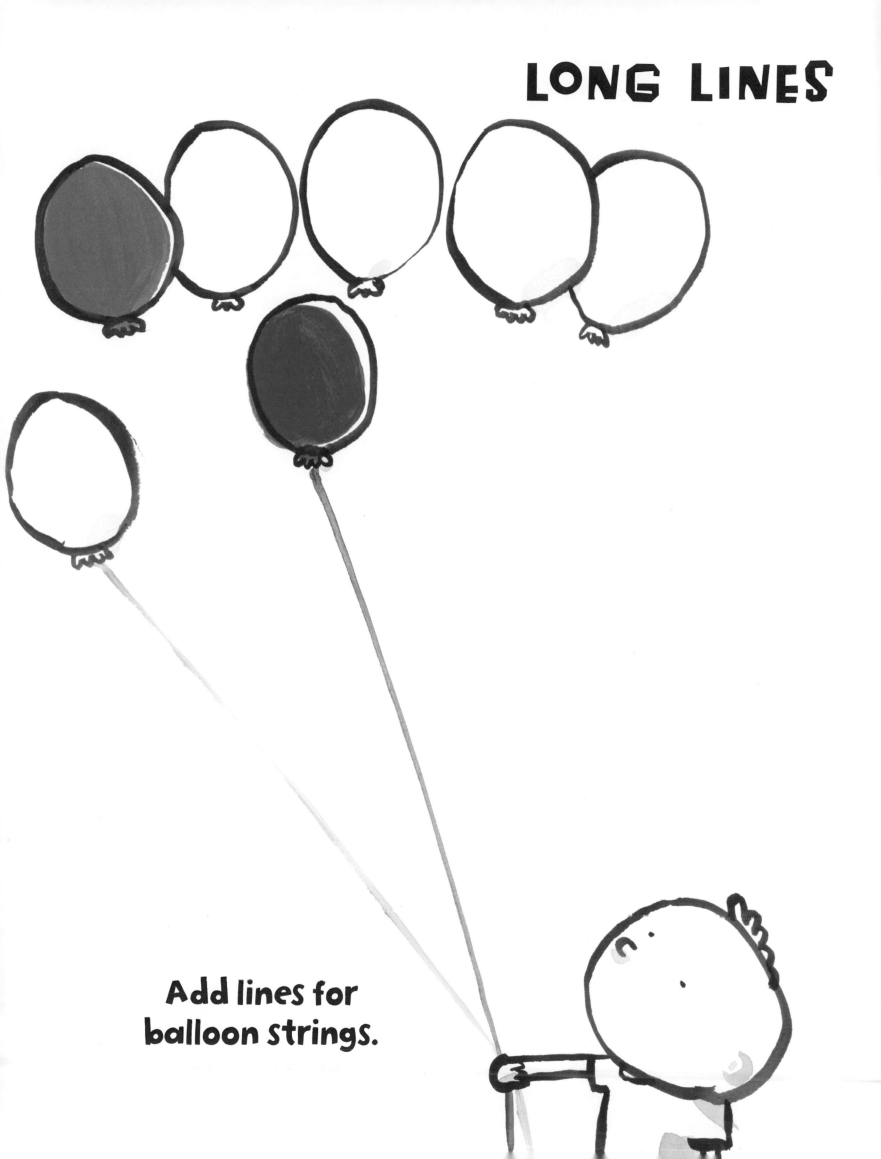

Add lines for
balloon strings.

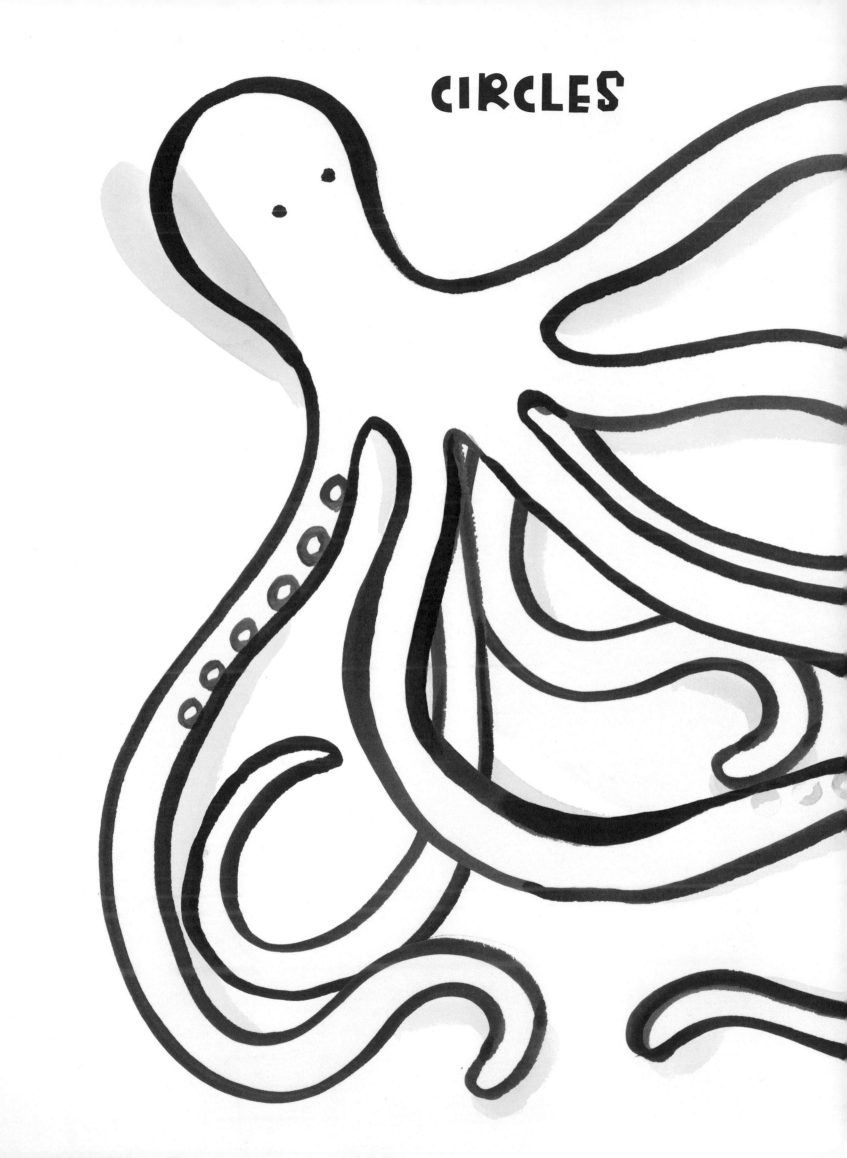

CIRCLES

Add suction cups to the tentacles.

SMALL CIRCLES

Add wheels.

STARS

Add stars.

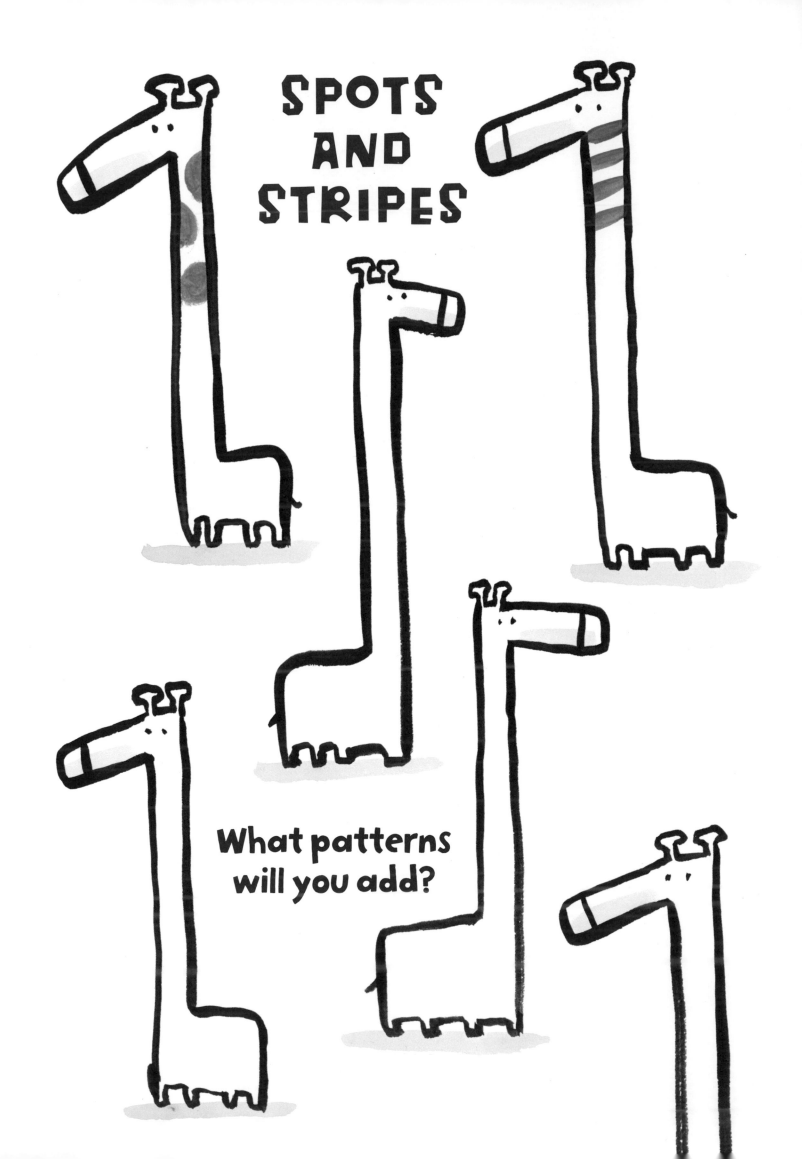

MORE
SPOTS

PATTERNS OF ALL KINDS

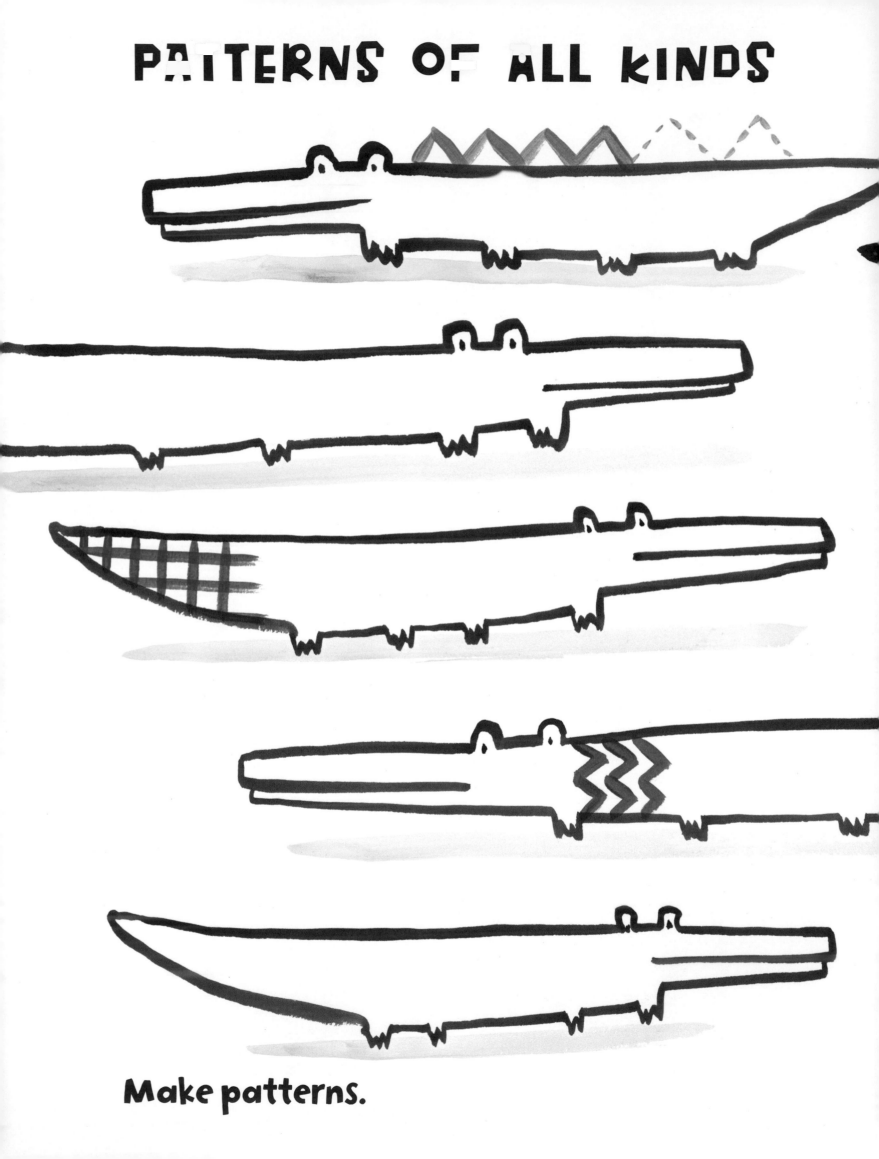

Make patterns.

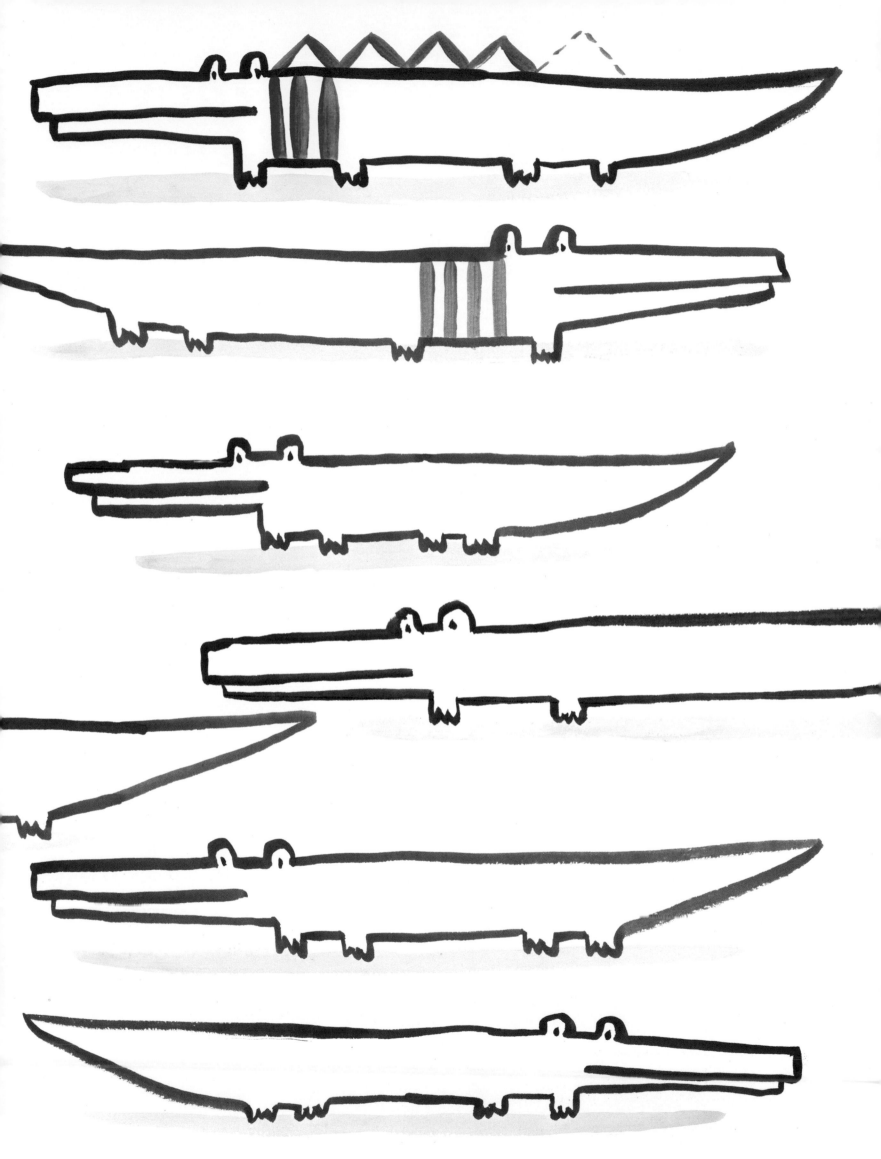

CRISS-CROSS

Finish the patterns.
Add scarves.

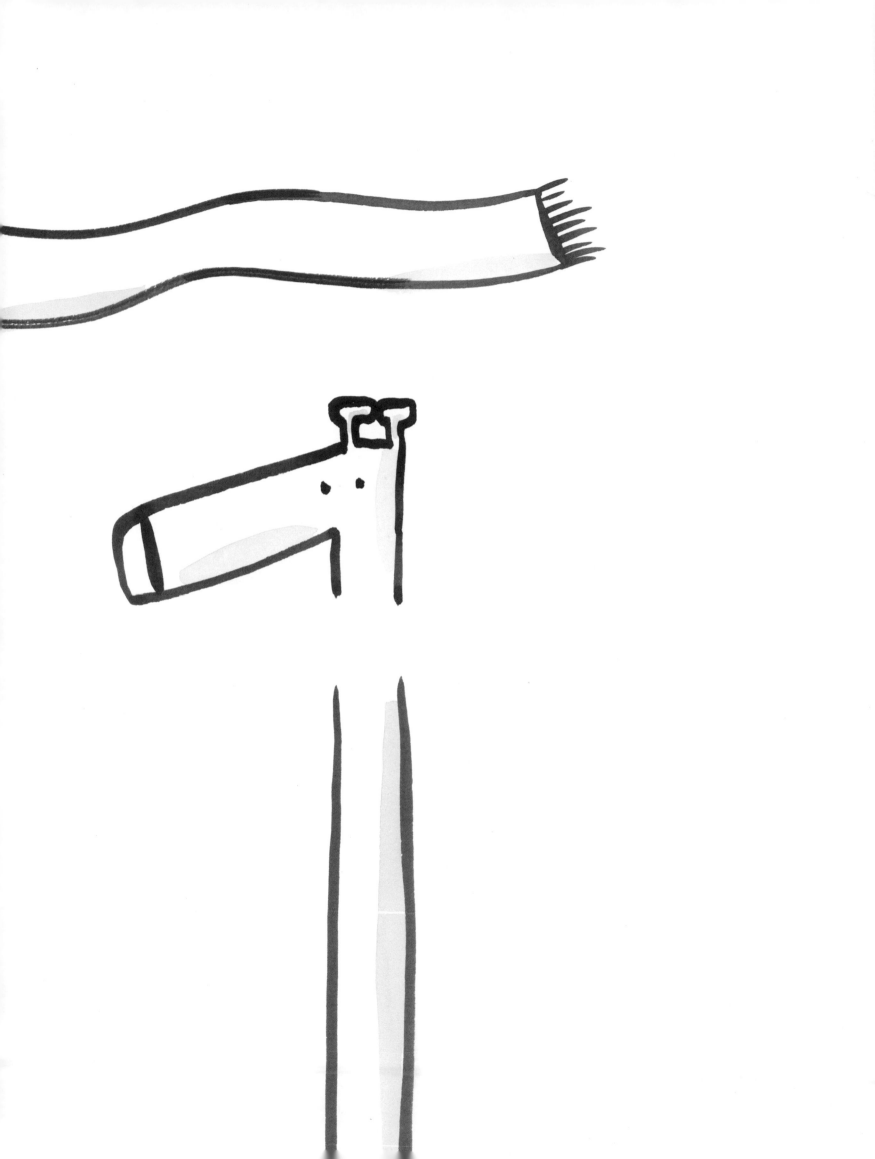

PATTERNS
IN THE
TREES

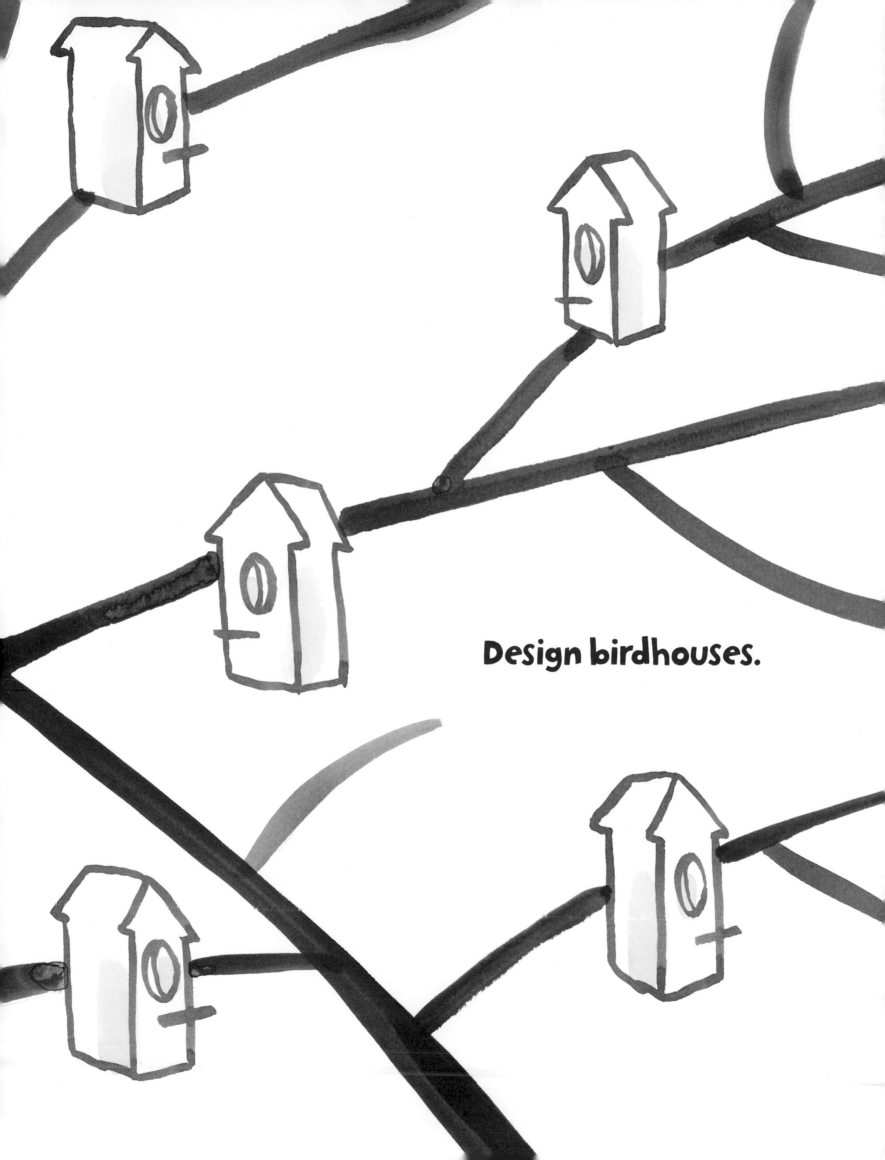

Design birdhouses.

TRIANGLES

Finish the patterns.

HISSSSS !

GARDEN PATTERNS

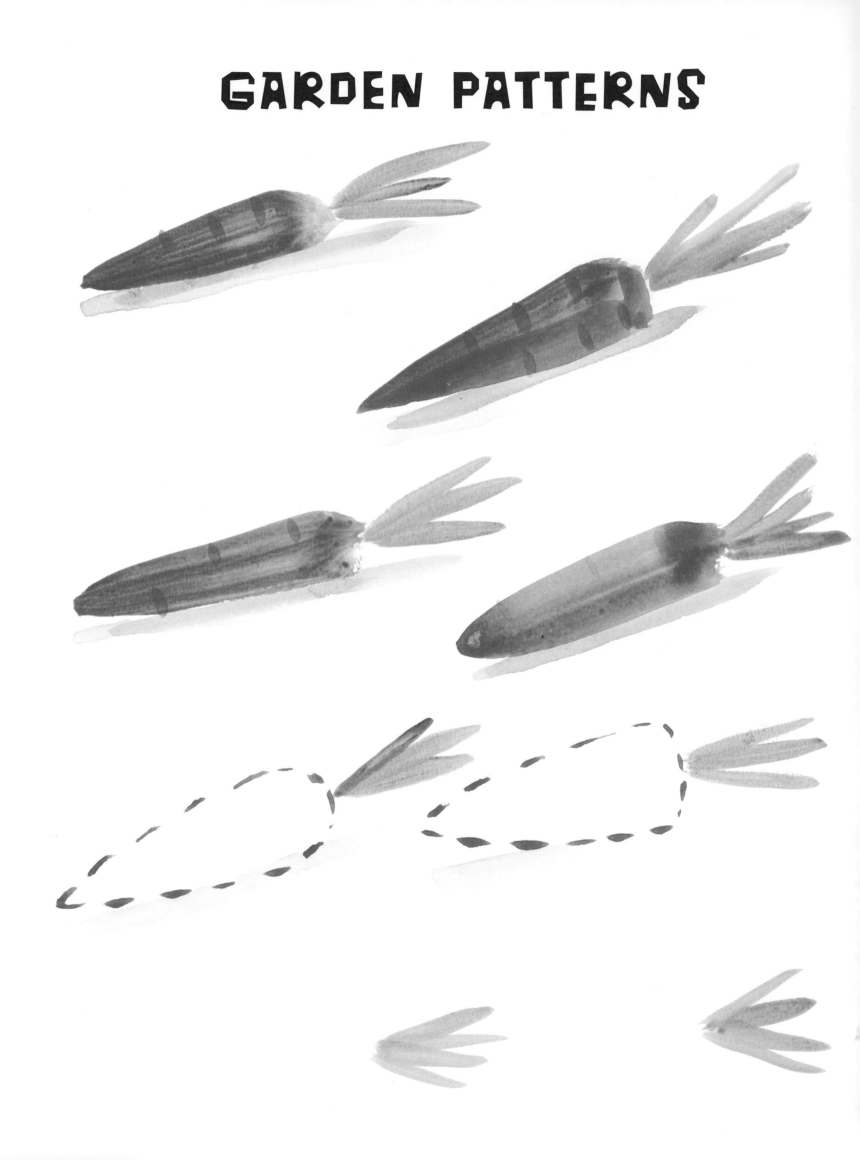

Finish the patterns.

STRIPES + SQUARES

Give the trucks stripes and cargo.

SPOTS

Give the elephant
more spots!

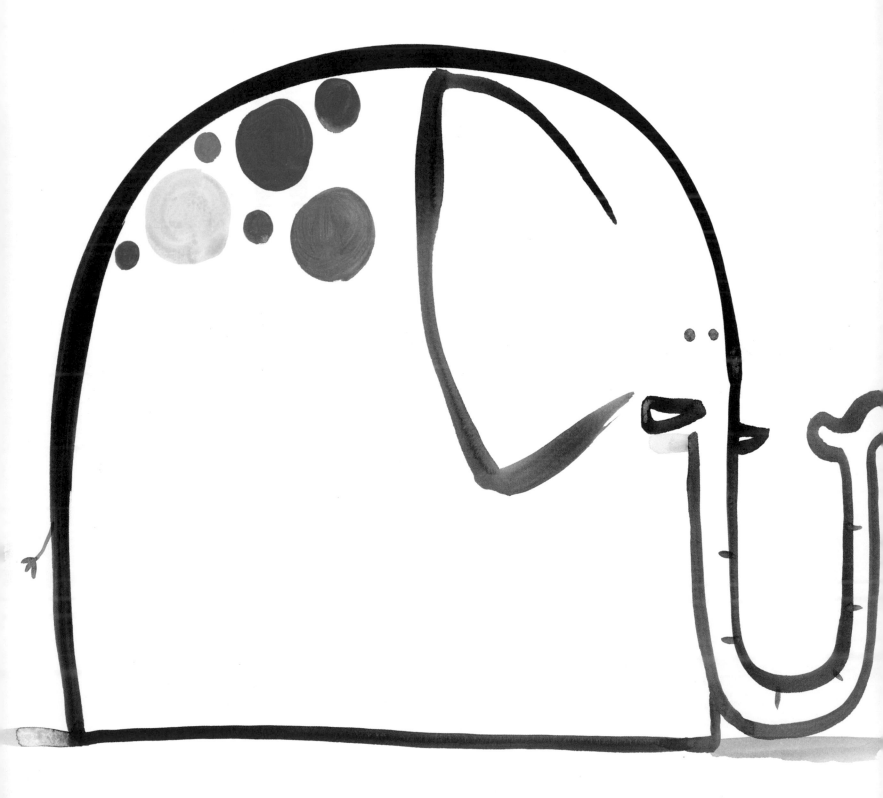

LOOPY LINE
Decorate this pillow for bedtime.

MORE SPOTS

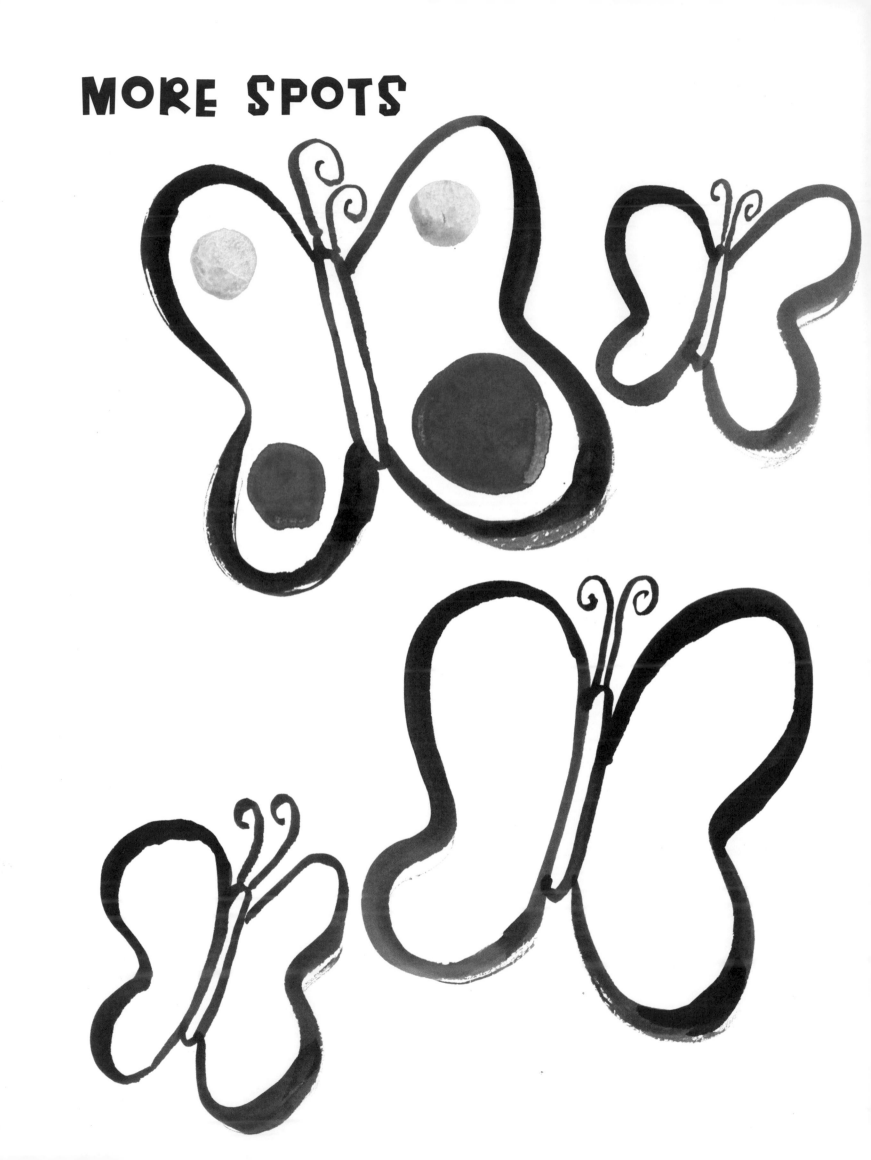

Give the butterflies more spots.

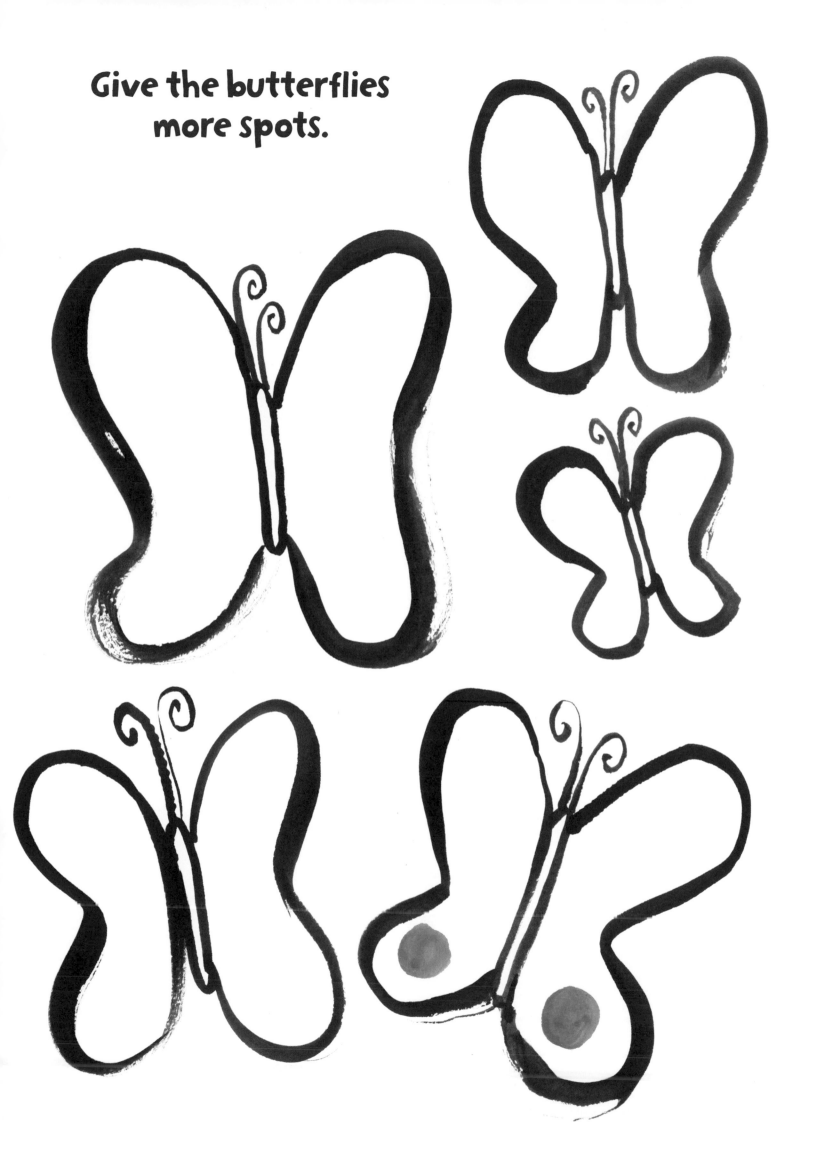

SCALES

Give the fish more scales.

CURVES + LOOPS

Give the planes
loopy trails.

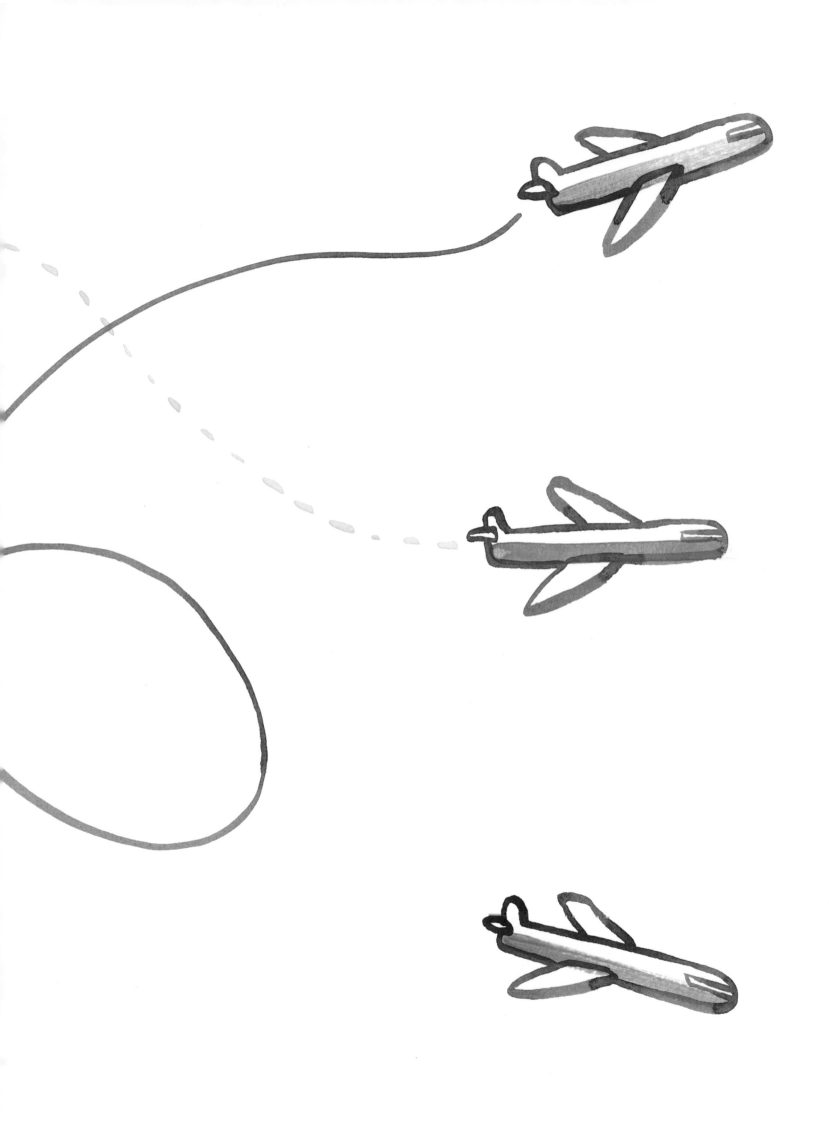

CURVY LINES

Give these mice
ears and tails.

SPIRALS

Give these snails shells.

BASKET WEAVE

Add patterns to the sweaters.

CURVES IN PAIRS

Add creepy, crawly legs!
How many did you add?
(A spider has eight legs.)

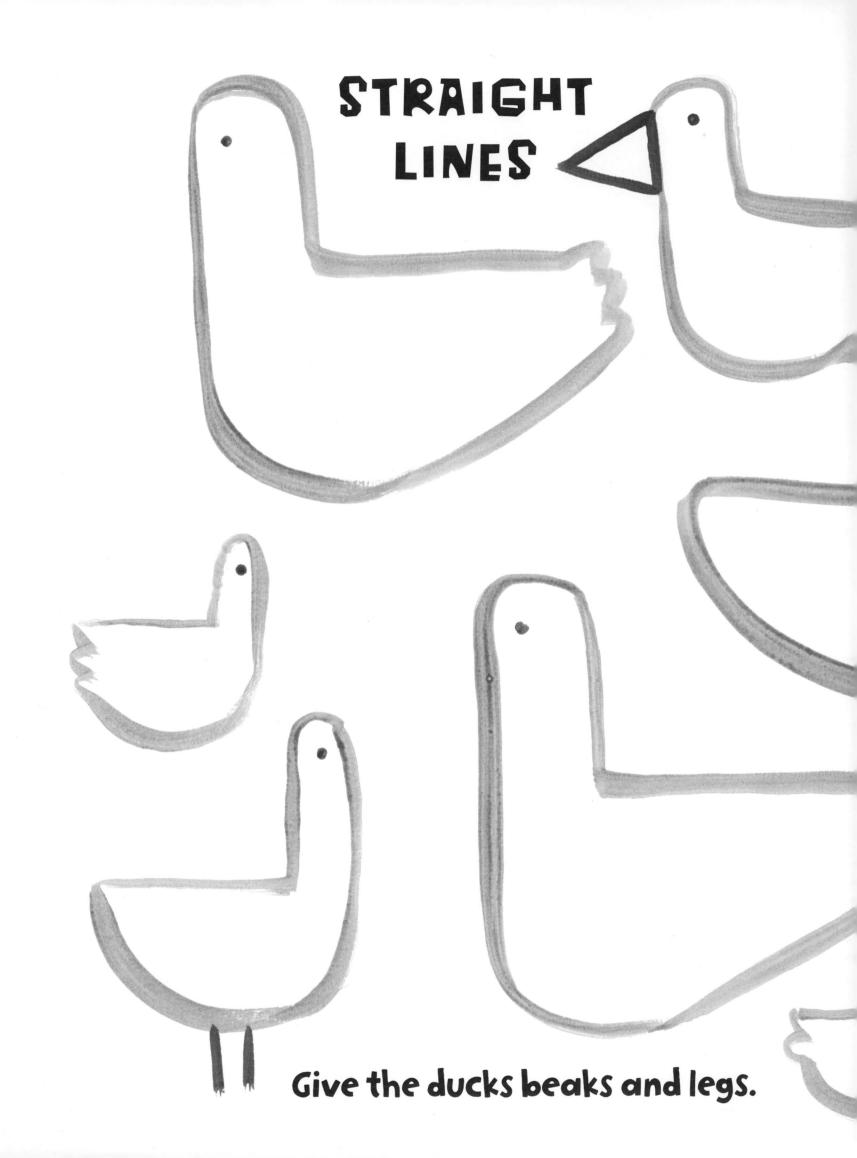

STRAIGHT LINES

Give the ducks beaks and legs.

TRIANGLES

OVALS

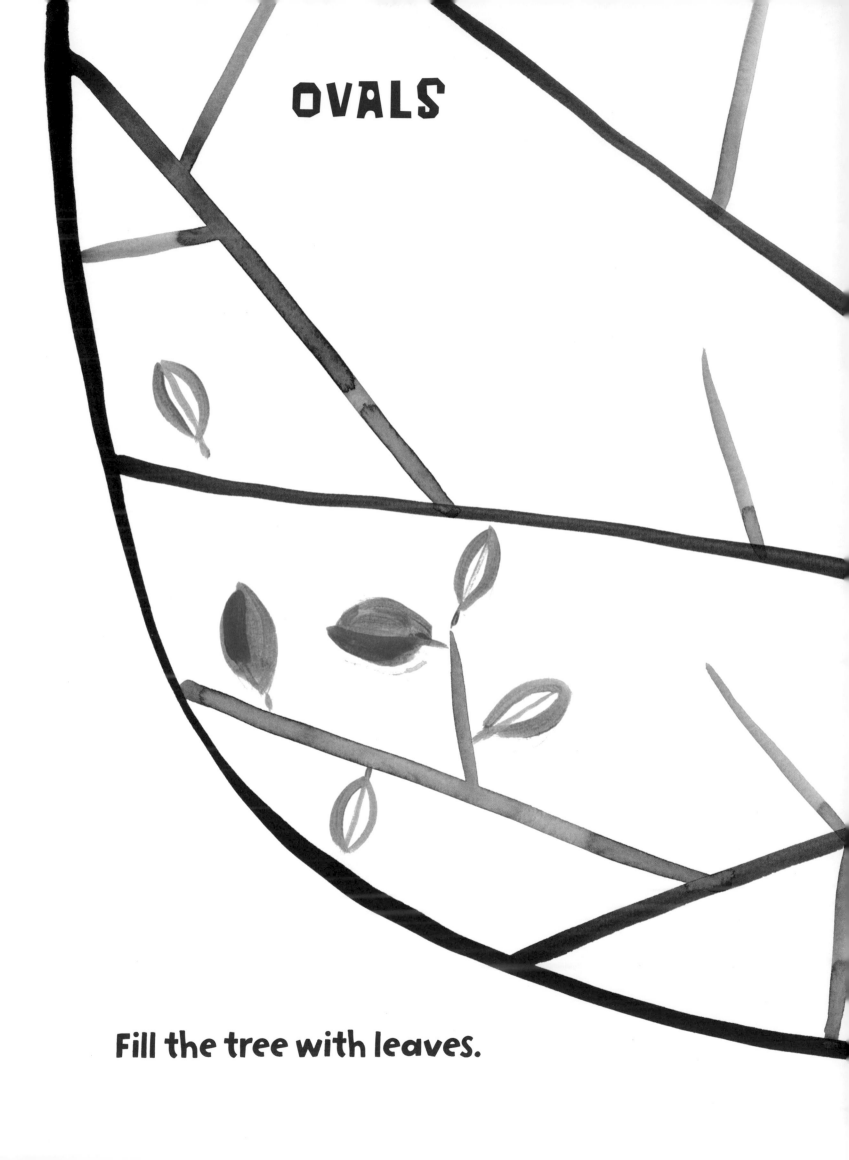

Fill the tree with leaves.

BUZZ! BUZZ! BUZZ!

Add wings and stripes.

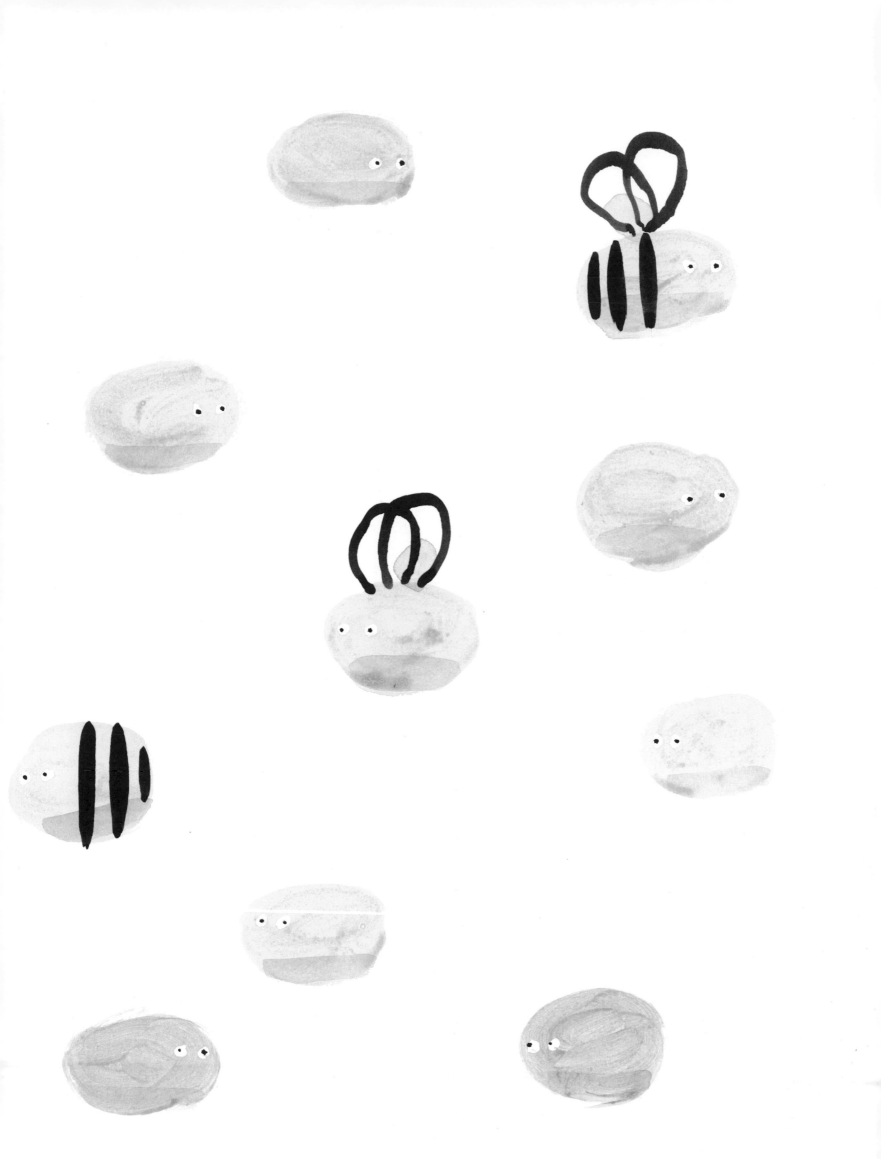

LINES THAT CROSS

Draw lines.

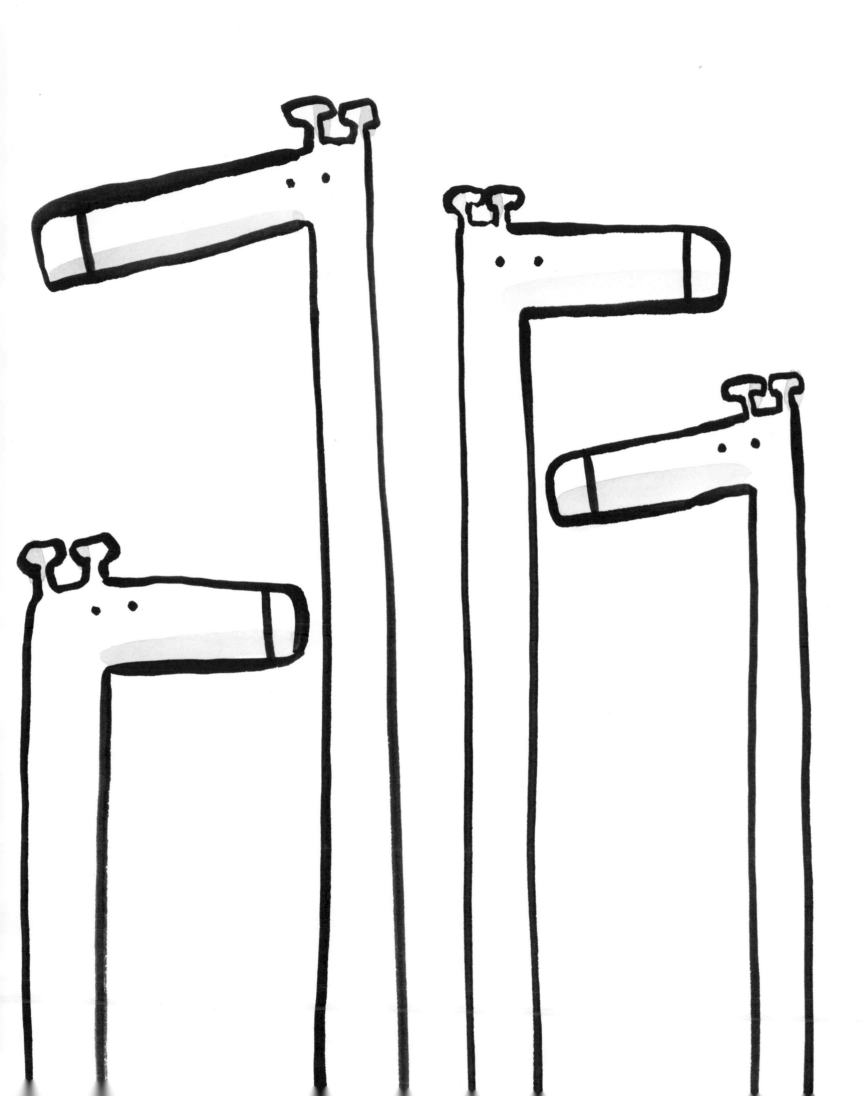

SHORT, THICK LINES

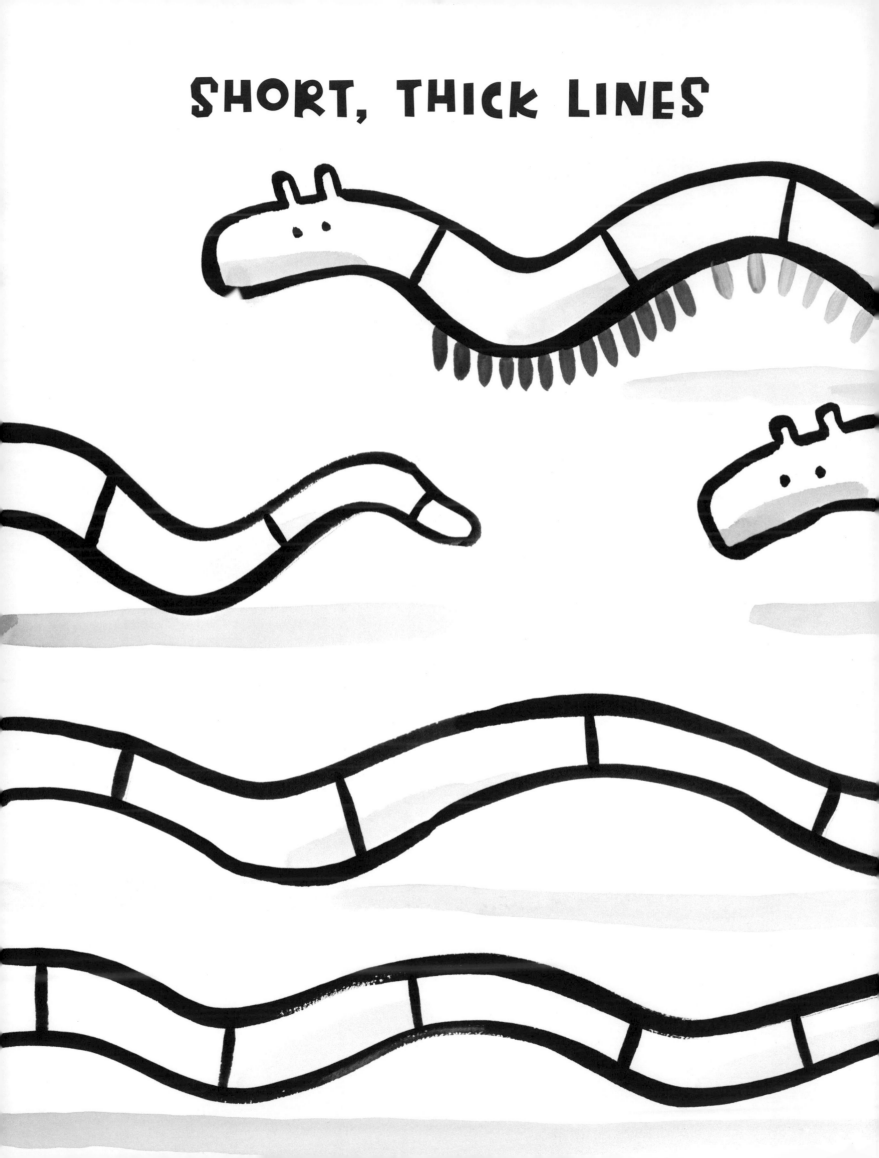

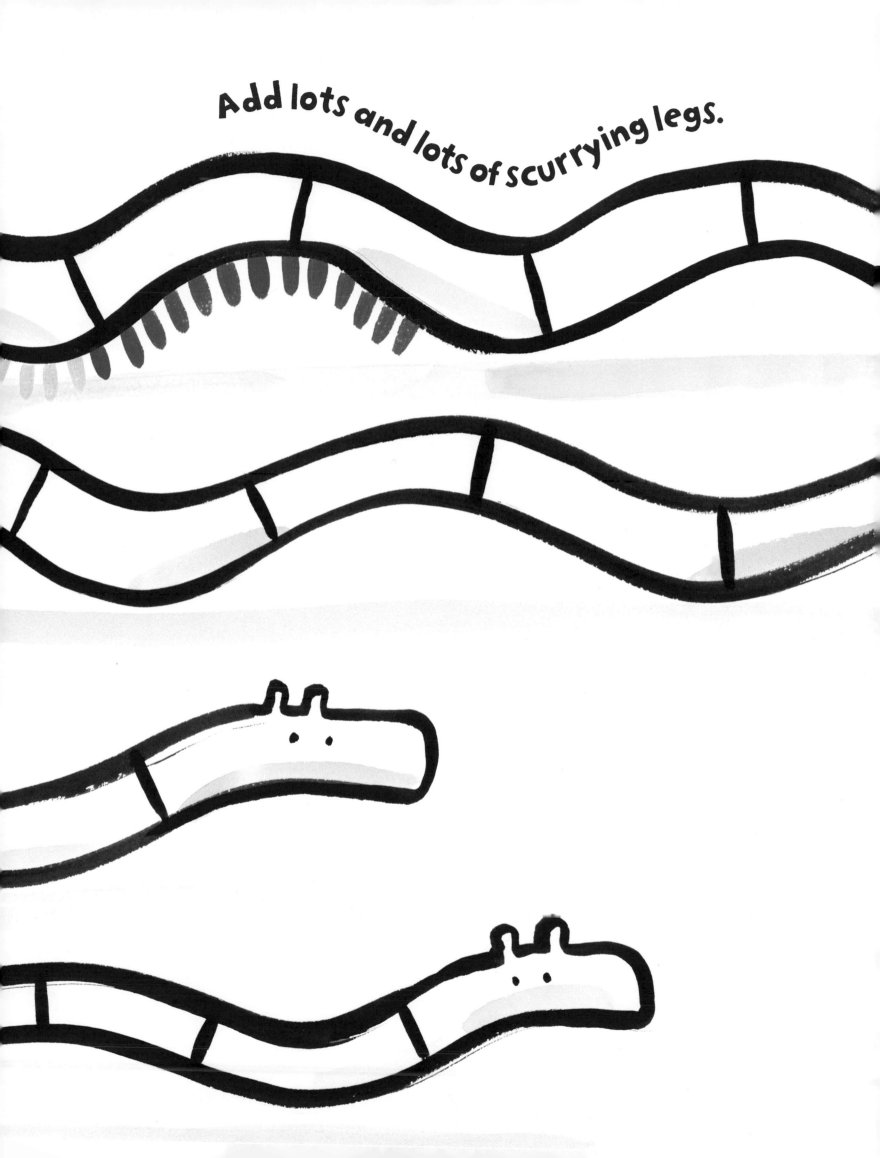

Add lots and lots of scurrying legs.

BIG CURVES

Finish the patterns.

MAKE YOUR OWN PATTERNS.

MAKE YOUR OWN PATTERNS.

MAKE YOUR OWN PATTERNS.